Inner Peace

Discover the Power of Mindfulness and Emotional Mastery
to Cultivate a Life of Inner Peace and Happiness: A Comprehensive Guide to Finding Balance and Fulfillment

Lance P. Richards

Inner Peace: Discover the Power of Mindfulness and Emotional Mastery to Cultivate a Life of Inner Peace and Happiness: A Comprehensive Guide to Finding Balance and Fulfillment

Table of Contents

01: Introduction: The Importance of Inner Peace

Inner peace is a concept that has been cherished by people from all cultures and beliefs throughout history. It is a state of calmness, serenity, and contentment that allows us to navigate life's challenges and obstacles with grace and ease. Inner peace is not just a fleeting feeling, but a deep and abiding sense of well-being that can sustain us through life's ups and downs. It is a key to finding balance and fulfillment in life, and a powerful tool for cultivating happiness and joy.

The importance of inner peace can be seen in our daily lives. We all experience stress and anxiety, and often struggle to find meaning and purpose in a world that can seem chaotic and overwhelming. We are constantly bombarded by distractions and external stimuli, making it difficult to focus and connect with our inner selves. In order to find peace and happiness, it is essential that we learn to quiet our minds, cultivate emotional intelligence, and connect with our deepest values and beliefs.

Mindfulness and emotional mastery are two essential components of cultivating inner peace. Mindfulness is the practice of paying attention to the present moment without judgment, allowing us to gain a deeper understanding of our thoughts and emotions. Emotional mastery involves gaining control over our reactions and emotions, and using them to enhance our lives rather than being controlled by them. These two practices are interrelated and complement each other, and when combined, they can help us cultivate a life of inner peace and happiness.

This book is a comprehensive guide to discovering the power of mindfulness and emotional mastery to cultivate inner peace. We will explore the latest research and practices in mindfulness, emotional intelligence, and well-being, and provide practical tips and exercises that you can use to cultivate inner peace in your daily life. Whether you are a beginner or an experienced practitioner, this book will provide you with the tools and insights you need to cultivate a life of balance and fulfillment.

In this chapter, we will delve into the importance of inner peace, and explore the ways in which mindfulness and emotional mastery can help us cultivate this essential state of being. We will also introduce the key concepts and practices that will be covered in this book, and provide an overview of

01: INTRODUCTION: THE IMPORTANCE OF INNER PEACE

what you can expect to learn as you read on.

By the end of this chapter, you will have a deeper understanding of the importance of inner peace, and why mindfulness and emotional mastery are essential components of cultivating this state of being. You will be inspired to embark on your own journey towards inner peace, and equipped with the tools and insights you need to make this journey a success.

02: Understanding Mindfulness: What It Is and How It Works

Mindfulness is a practice that has been gaining popularity in recent years, and for good reason. It is a simple yet powerful tool for cultivating inner peace and improving our overall well-being. But what exactly is mindfulness, and how does it work?

Mindfulness is the practice of paying attention to the present moment, without judgment or distraction. It involves becoming aware of our thoughts, feelings, and sensations, and accepting them without trying to change or control them. This allows us to gain a deeper understanding of our inner selves and the world around us, and to cultivate a greater sense of inner peace and happiness.

The concept of mindfulness has its roots in ancient Buddhist meditation practices, but it has been adapted and modified to fit into a modern context. It is now widely recognized as a valuable tool for reducing stress and anxiety, improving mental clarity and focus, and cultivating a greater sense of well-being.

One of the key benefits of mindfulness is that it helps us to become more aware of our thoughts and emotions, and to gain a deeper understanding of the ways in which they impact our lives. By becoming more mindful, we can begin to see the patterns and tendencies in our thinking, and gain greater control over our reactions and emotions. This allows us to make positive changes in our lives, and to cultivate a greater sense of inner peace and happiness.

Another key benefit of mindfulness is that it helps us to develop greater emotional intelligence. Emotional intelligence involves understanding and managing our own emotions, as well as being able to understand and respond to the emotions of others. By becoming more mindful, we can develop a greater ability to regulate our emotions and reactions, and to communicate more effectively with others.

The practice of mindfulness is relatively simple, but it can be challenging to stick with in the beginning. It involves setting aside time each day to focus on the present moment, and to pay attention to our thoughts and emotions. This can be done through meditation, deep breathing exercises, or simply paying attention to the sensations in our bodies. The key is to be patient and persistent, and to approach the practice with an open mind and a willingness to learn.

In this chapter, we will delve deeper into the concept of mindfulness, and explore the ways in which it can help us cultivate inner peace and happiness. We will also provide practical tips and exercises that you can use to begin incorporating mindfulness into your daily life. By the end of this chapter, you will have a deeper understanding of what mindfulness is, and how it can help you cultivate inner peace and happiness.

So, if you're ready to learn more about mindfulness and how it can help you cultivate inner peace, let's get started!

03: Emotional Mastery: How to Gain Control Over Your Emotions

Emotions are a natural and important part of our lives, but they can also be a source of stress and discomfort. When we feel overwhelmed by our emotions, it can be difficult to think clearly and make decisions that are in our best interest. That's why it's so important to develop emotional mastery - the ability to regulate our emotions and respond to them in a healthy, productive way.

Emotional mastery involves several key skills, including emotional awareness, emotional regulation, and emotional intelligence. By becoming more emotionally aware, we can gain a deeper understanding of our own emotions, and the ways in which they impact our lives. This allows us to make positive changes in our lives, and to cultivate greater inner peace and happiness.

Emotional regulation involves learning to control our emotional responses, so that we can avoid becoming overwhelmed by negative emotions like anger, fear, and anxiety. This can involve using mindfulness and other strategies to help us stay calm and focused in the face of challenging situations.

03: EMOTIONAL MASTERY: HOW TO GAIN CONTROL OVER YOUR EMOTIONS

Emotional intelligence involves understanding and managing our own emotions, as well as being able to understand and respond to the emotions of others. This can involve developing better communication skills, learning to identify and respond to the emotions of others, and becoming more self-aware and introspective.

So, how can you begin to develop emotional mastery? The first step is to become more mindful of your emotions, and to pay attention to the ways in which they impact your thoughts and behavior. This can involve practicing mindfulness exercises, journaling about your emotions, or simply taking time each day to reflect on your feelings.

Another important step is to develop healthy coping mechanisms for dealing with stress and anxiety. This can involve taking breaks from stressful situations, engaging in physical activity or mindfulness practices, or seeking support from friends, family, or a mental health professional.

It's also important to learn to manage your thoughts and beliefs, as these can have a significant impact on your emotional well-being. Negative thoughts and beliefs can contribute to feelings of anxiety and stress, while positive thoughts and beliefs can help us feel more confident and optimistic.

Finally, it's important to develop good communication skills, so that you can effectively express your emotions and respond to the emotions of others. This can involve learning to listen actively, using "I" statements to express your feelings, and avoiding blaming or accusing language.

In this chapter, we will delve deeper into the concept of emotional mastery, and explore the ways in which it can help you cultivate inner peace and happiness. We will also provide practical tips and exercises that you can use to begin developing your emotional mastery skills. By the end of this chapter, you will have a deeper understanding of how to gain control over your emotions and to cultivate a life of inner peace and happiness.

So, if you're ready to learn more about emotional mastery and how it can help you cultivate inner peace, let's get started!

04: The Science of Inner Peace: The Latest Research on Mindfulness and Emotional Intelligence

In recent years, there has been a growing body of scientific evidence demonstrating the benefits of mindfulness and emotional intelligence for cultivating inner peace and happiness. This research has shown that mindfulness practices can help to reduce stress and anxiety, improve our ability to regulate our emotions, and enhance our overall well-being.

One of the key findings in this field is that mindfulness and emotional intelligence are related to changes in brain structure and function. For example, studies have shown that mindfulness practices can increase the size of the prefrontal cortex, which is responsible for executive functions like decision making, planning, and problem solving. Additionally, mindfulness has been shown to increase the connectivity between the prefrontal cortex and the amygdala, which is responsible for our emotional responses.

Another key finding is that mindfulness and emotional intelligence can help to improve our resilience, or the ability to bounce back from adversity. For example, studies have shown that mindfulness practices can increase our ability to cope with stress and negative emotions, and to maintain our emotional balance in the face of adversity. Additionally, research has demonstrated that individuals with high emotional intelligence are better able to regulate their emotions, and to respond to stressful situations in a more adaptive way.

There is also growing evidence that mindfulness and emotional intelligence can have positive effects on our physical health. For example, studies have shown that mindfulness practices can lower levels of stress hormones, and reduce symptoms of anxiety and depression. Additionally, research has demonstrated that individuals with high emotional intelligence are more likely to engage in healthy behaviors, like regular exercise, and to make healthier lifestyle choices.

In this chapter, we will examine the latest research on mindfulness and emotional intelligence, and explore the ways in which these practices can help to cultivate inner peace and happiness. We will also look at the various techniques and approaches that have been developed to help individuals develop mindfulness and emotional intelligence, and will provide practical tips and exercises that you can use to start developing these skills.

So, if you're ready to learn more about the science of inner peace, and to discover the latest research on mindfulness and emotional intelligence, let's dive in!

05: The Benefits of Mindfulness and Emotional Mastery

Introduction:

Inner peace and happiness are among the most sought-after experiences in life, yet they can often seem elusive and out of reach. Many people struggle with feelings of stress, anxiety, and negativity, which can lead to a sense of unhappiness and dissatisfaction with life. However, it is possible to cultivate a life of inner peace and happiness, even in the midst of challenging circumstances. One of the most powerful ways to achieve this is through the practices of mindfulness and emotional mastery.

Mindfulness:

Mindfulness is a mental state achieved by focusing one's awareness on the present moment, while calmly acknowledging and accepting one's feelings, thoughts, and sensations. By bringing awareness to the present moment, mindfulness helps us to escape from the constant barrage of negative thoughts and worries that often undermine our peace of mind. Instead, we are able to simply observe our thoughts and feelings without judgment, which helps us to cultivate a sense of calm and detachment.

There are many benefits to practicing mindfulness, including reduced stress and anxiety, improved mood, enhanced focus and concentration, and greater overall well-being. Research has shown that mindfulness practices can help to regulate emotions, reduce feelings of depression, and even boost the immune system.

Emotional Mastery:

Emotional mastery is the ability to understand and manage our emotions in a healthy and constructive way. This involves learning to identify and understand our emotions, as well as recognizing and managing the triggers that cause them. By developing emotional mastery, we are better equipped to navigate the ups and downs of life with grace and equanimity.

Some of the benefits of emotional mastery include improved relationships, enhanced resilience and coping skills, greater overall well-being, and a reduced risk of depression and anxiety. By learning to manage our emotions in a healthy way, we are better equipped to maintain inner peace and happiness, even in the face of challenging circumstances.

Combining Mindfulness and Emotional Mastery:

When combined, mindfulness and emotional mastery can be a powerful force for positive change in our lives. By practicing mindfulness, we can bring awareness to our thoughts and feelings, which helps us to develop a deeper understanding of our emotions. At the same time, by developing emotional mastery, we can learn to manage our emotions in a healthy way, which helps us to maintain inner peace and happiness even in the face of adversity.

Conclusion:

Inner peace and happiness are within reach for all of us, and the practices of mindfulness and emotional mastery can help us to achieve these important goals. Whether you are looking to improve your relationships, reduce stress and anxiety, or simply cultivate a greater sense of well-being, these practices can help you to create a life filled with balance and fulfillment. So why wait? Start your journey to inner peace and happiness today, and discover the powerful

05: THE BENEFITS OF MINDFULNESS AND EMO-TIONAL MASTERY

benefits of mindfulness and emotional mastery.

06: Understanding the Mind-Body Connection: How Thoughts and Emotions Affect Physical Health

Introduction:

The connection between the mind and the body is a complex and intricate one, and it is widely recognized that our thoughts and emotions can have a significant impact on our physical health. In fact, it is well established that stress, anxiety, and negative emotions can contribute to a range of physical health problems, including headaches, digestive issues, and even chronic conditions such as heart disease and stroke. Conversely, a positive outlook and the cultivation of inner peace and happiness can have a profound impact on our overall well-being, leading to improved physical health and vitality.

The Science of the Mind-Body Connection:

The science of the mind-body connection is rooted in the understanding that our thoughts and emotions play a crucial role in regulating the functions of our bodies. For example, when we experience stress or anxiety, our bodies respond by releasing stress hormones such as cortisol and adrenaline. These hormones trigger the "fight or flight" response, which prepares our bodies for physical action. However, if the stress response is activated too frequently, or for too long, it can cause physical and mental exhaustion, as well as contributing to the development of physical health problems.

On the other hand, positive thoughts and emotions can lead to the release of feel-good hormones such as dopamine and serotonin, which can help to regulate our mood, improve our mental clarity, and enhance our overall well-being. In this way, our thoughts and emotions can have a direct impact on the functions of our bodies, affecting everything from our immune system to our heart rate and breathing patterns.

The Power of Mindfulness and Emotional Mastery:

Mindfulness and emotional mastery are powerful tools for improving the mind-body connection, as they help us to bring awareness to our thoughts and emotions, and to understand and manage them in a healthy and constructive way. By practicing mindfulness, we can learn to identify and acknowledge our emotions, rather than allowing them to control us. This allows us to regulate our stress response, reducing the risk of physical health problems associated with chronic stress and anxiety.

Emotional mastery, on the other hand, helps us to develop the skills needed to manage our emotions in a healthy way, reducing the impact of negative emotions on our physical health. By learning to recognize and manage the triggers that cause negative emotions, we can reduce the frequency and intensity of these emotions, leading to a greater sense of well-being and improved physical health.

The Benefits of Improving the Mind-Body Connection:

The benefits of improving the mind-body connection are numerous and wide-ranging, and can include reduced stress and anxiety, improved mood, enhanced mental clarity and focus, and a reduced risk of physical health problems. By learning to regulate our thoughts and emotions, we can experience a greater sense of inner peace and happiness, leading to improved physical health and vitality.

06: UNDERSTANDING THE MIND-BODY CONNECTION: HOW THOUGHTS AND EMOTIONS AFFECT PHYSICAL HEALTH

In addition, by cultivating mindfulness and emotional mastery, we can develop a greater understanding of the connection between our thoughts and emotions and the functions of our bodies. This knowledge can help us to make more informed decisions about our health, leading to improved overall well-being and longevity.

Conclusion:

The connection between the mind and the body is a complex and powerful one, and it is essential that we understand and harness this connection if we are to cultivate inner peace and happiness, and achieve optimal physical health and well-being. Through the practices of mindfulness and emotional mastery, we can improve our mind-body connection, reducing the impact of stress and anxiety, and enhancing our overall well-being and vitality. So why wait? Start your journey to a healthier, happier life today, and discover the power of the mind-body connection.

07: Overcoming Negative Thoughts and Limiting Beliefs

Introduction:

Negative thoughts and limiting beliefs are common obstacles to inner peace and happiness, and can hold us back from realizing our full potential. These thoughts and beliefs can take many forms, from self-doubt and insecurity, to fears and phobias, and can impact all aspects of our lives, from our relationships to our careers and personal goals.

However, with the right tools and techniques, it is possible to overcome negative thoughts and limiting beliefs, and to cultivate a life of inner peace and happiness. In this chapter, we will explore the causes of negative thoughts and limiting beliefs, and outline practical strategies for overcoming these obstacles and achieving greater balance and fulfillment in life.

The Causes of Negative Thoughts and Limiting Beliefs:

Negative thoughts and limiting beliefs often stem from past experiences, such as childhood traumas or relationship difficulties, and can be reinforced by negative self-talk, social comparisons, and other external factors. These thoughts and beliefs can also be perpetuated by our subconscious mind, which can hold on to negative patterns of thinking even after we have consciously made an effort to change them.

However, despite their deep-rooted nature, negative thoughts and limiting beliefs are not permanent, and can be overcome with the right approach. By identifying and addressing the underlying causes of these thoughts and beliefs, and by developing new, positive patterns of thinking, it is possible to break free from their hold and cultivate a life of inner peace and happiness.

The Power of Mindfulness and Emotional Mastery:

Mindfulness and emotional mastery are powerful tools for overcoming negative thoughts and limiting beliefs, as they help us to bring awareness to our thoughts and emotions, and to understand and manage them in a healthy and constructive way. By practicing mindfulness, we can learn to identify and acknowledge our negative thoughts and beliefs, rather than allowing them to control us. This allows us to challenge and reframe these thoughts, reducing their im-

07: OVERCOMING NEGATIVE THOUGHTS AND LIMITING BELIEFS

pact on our lives.

Emotional mastery, on the other hand, helps us to develop the skills needed to manage our emotions in a healthy way, reducing the impact of negative thoughts and beliefs on our well-being. By learning to recognize and manage the triggers that cause negative emotions, we can reduce the frequency and intensity of these thoughts and beliefs, leading to a greater sense of inner peace and happiness.

Overcoming Negative Thoughts and Limiting Beliefs: Practical Strategies

– Identifying Negative Thoughts and Limiting Beliefs: The first step in overcoming negative thoughts and limiting beliefs is to identify and acknowledge them. This can be done through mindfulness practices, such as journaling or meditation, or through self-reflection and introspection.

– Reframing Negative Thoughts: Once we have identified our negative thoughts and limiting beliefs, we can begin to reframe them in a more positive light. This can be done by questioning the evidence for these thoughts, seeking out alternative perspectives, and focusing on our strengths and accomplishments.

– Developing Positive Patterns of Thinking: To overcome negative thoughts and limiting beliefs, it is essential to develop positive patterns of thinking that support inner peace and happiness. This can be done through practices such as gratitude journaling, positive affirmations, and visualization.

– Practicing Emotional Mastery: Emotional mastery involves developing the skills needed to manage our emotions in a healthy way, reducing the impact of negative thoughts and beliefs on our well-being. This can be done through techniques such as cognitive-behavioral therapy, mindfulness-based stress reduction, and emotional intelligence training.

– Seeking Support: Overcoming negative thoughts and limiting beliefs can be challenging, and seeking support from friends, family, or a mental health professional can be an important part of the process. Talking to someone you trust and who understands your situation can provide a sounding board for your thoughts and feelings, and can help you to develop new perspectives and coping strategies.

07: OVERCOMING NEGATIVE THOUGHTS AND LIMITING BELIEFS

– Building Resilience: Resilience is the ability to bounce back from adversity, and is an important factor in overcoming negative thoughts and limiting beliefs. This can be developed through practices such as exercise, meditation, and developing a strong support network.

– Taking Action: Finally, taking action towards your goals and aspirations can be a powerful way to overcome negative thoughts and limiting beliefs. This can help to increase self-confidence, provide a sense of accomplishment, and create a positive feedback loop of positive thinking and behavior.

Conclusion:

Negative thoughts and limiting beliefs are common obstacles to inner peace and happiness, but they are not permanent and can be overcome with the right approach. By combining mindfulness and emotional mastery, and by implementing practical strategies for overcoming these obstacles, it is possible to cultivate a life of inner peace and happiness, and to realize your full potential.

Remember, the process of overcoming negative thoughts and limiting beliefs takes time, patience, and persistence, but the rewards are well worth the effort. By developing new patterns of thinking and behavior, and by seeking support when needed, you can create a more fulfilling and balanced life, filled with inner peace and happiness.

08: Finding Balance in a Busy World: Tips for Cultivating Inner Peace in Daily Life

Introduction:

In today's fast-paced world, it can be challenging to find balance and cultivate inner peace. With so many demands on our time and attention, it can be difficult to prioritize self-care and maintain a sense of calm amidst the chaos. However, it is essential to make time for inner peace and well-being, as this can have a profound impact on our overall happiness and satisfaction in life.

In this chapter, we will explore some tips for finding balance and cultivating inner peace in daily life. From mindfulness practices to time management techniques, these strategies can help you to create more space for inner peace, regardless of the demands and distractions of daily life.

– Mindfulness Practices: Mindfulness is a powerful tool for finding balance and cultivating inner peace. Incorporating mindfulness practices into your daily routine, such as meditation, breathing exercises, or yoga, can help you to stay grounded and centered, even in the midst of busy days.

08: FINDING BALANCE IN A BUSY WORLD: TIPS FOR CULTIVATING INNER PEACE IN DAILY LIFE

– Prioritize Self-Care: Making time for self-care is crucial for maintaining inner peace. This might include activities such as exercise, reading, or taking a relaxing bath. By making self-care a priority, you can help to reduce stress and anxiety, and cultivate a sense of inner peace.

– Time Management: Effective time management is key to finding balance in a busy world. This can involve prioritizing tasks, delegating responsibilities, and avoiding time-wasters. By managing your time more effectively, you can create more space for inner peace and well-being.

– Connect with Nature: Spending time in nature can have a calming and rejuvenating effect on the mind and body. This might involve activities such as hiking, gardening, or simply taking a walk in the park. By connecting with nature, you can cultivate a sense of inner peace and find balance in a busy world.

– Mindful Communication: Mindful communication is an important aspect of finding balance and cultivating inner peace. This involves being present and attentive in conversations, and practicing active listening. By communicating mindfully, you can reduce stress and build stronger relationships, which can help to create a sense of inner peace.

– Cultivate Gratitude: Cultivating gratitude is a powerful way to find balance and cultivate inner peace. By focusing on the things you are thankful for, you can shift your focus away from negative thoughts and emotions, and cultivate a sense of appreciation and contentment.

– Find a Support Network: Having a support network can be invaluable in finding balance and cultivating inner peace. Whether it is friends, family, or a community of like-minded individuals, having a support network can provide a source of encouragement and inspiration, and help you to maintain a sense of inner peace even in challenging times.

Conclusion:

Finding balance and cultivating inner peace in a busy world requires effort and dedication, but the rewards are well worth it. By incorporating mindfulness practices, prioritizing self-care, managing time effectively, and seeking support, you can create more space for inner peace and happiness, and find balance in your daily life.

08: FINDING BALANCE IN A BUSY WORLD: TIPS FOR CULTIVATING INNER PEACE IN DAILY LIFE

Remember, cultivating inner peace is a lifelong journey, and it is important to be patient and persistent in your efforts. By taking small steps every day, you can create a more balanced and fulfilling life, filled with inner peace and happiness.

09: The Power of Gratitude: Why Saying "Thank You" Matters

Introduction:

Gratitude is one of the most powerful and transformative emotions we can experience. It has the ability to shift our focus from what is lacking in our lives to what we already have, and this can have a profound impact on our well-being and happiness. In this chapter, we will explore the power of gratitude and why saying "thank you" matters.

– The Benefits of Gratitude: Gratitude has been shown to have a number of benefits for our well-being, including improved mental health, increased happiness, and reduced stress and anxiety. By focusing on what we are thankful for, we can shift our focus away from negative thoughts and emotions, and cultivate a sense of inner peace and contentment.

– Gratitude Increases Happiness: Research has shown that practicing gratitude can increase happiness and satisfaction in life. By focusing on what we are thankful for, we can increase our positive emotions and experience greater joy and fulfillment.

09: THE POWER OF GRATITUDE: WHY SAYING "THANK YOU" MATTERS

– Gratitude Reduces Stress and Anxiety: Gratitude can also help to reduce stress and anxiety. By focusing on what we are thankful for, we can shift our focus away from negative thoughts and emotions, and cultivate a sense of calm and well-being.

– Gratitude Strengthens Relationships: Practicing gratitude can also have a positive impact on our relationships. By expressing appreciation and thanks, we can build stronger connections with others, and cultivate a sense of community and support.

– Gratitude Improves Mental Health: Gratitude has been shown to have a positive impact on mental health, including reducing symptoms of depression and anxiety. By focusing on what we are thankful for, we can improve our overall well-being and happiness.

– Cultivating Gratitude in Daily Life: Cultivating gratitude in daily life requires effort and dedication, but the rewards are well worth it. Some simple ways to incorporate gratitude into your life include keeping a gratitude journal, writing thank-you notes, or simply taking a moment each day to reflect on what you are thankful for.

09: THE POWER OF GRATITUDE: WHY SAYING "THANK YOU" MATTERS

Conclusion:

Saying "thank you" is a simple yet powerful act that can have a profound impact on our well-being and happiness. By focusing on what we are thankful for, we can shift our focus away from negative thoughts and emotions, and cultivate a sense of inner peace and contentment. Whether it's through daily gratitude practices, expressing appreciation to others, or simply taking a moment each day to reflect on what we are thankful for, the power of gratitude is one that should not be underestimated.

So, take some time today to reflect on what you are thankful for, and let the power of gratitude work its magic in your life. By focusing on gratitude, you can cultivate a sense of inner peace and happiness, and experience the many benefits that come with it.

10: Mindful Breathing: A Simple but Effective Practice for Inner Peace

Mindful breathing is a simple but effective practice for cultivating inner peace and well-being. By focusing on the breath, we can quiet the mind, reduce stress and anxiety, and cultivate a sense of calm and inner peace. In this chapter, we will explore the benefits of mindful breathing and how you can incorporate it into your daily life.

– The Benefits of Mindful Breathing: Mindful breathing has been shown to have a number of benefits for our well-being, including reduced stress and anxiety, improved focus and concentration, and increased feelings of calm and inner peace. By focusing on the breath, we can bring our awareness to the present moment, and quiet the mind, reducing the impact of negative thoughts and emotions.

– How to Practice Mindful Breathing: Practicing mindful breathing is simple and can be done anywhere, at any time. Simply find a comfortable seat, close your eyes, and focus on your breath, noticing the sensation of the air as it enters and leaves your body. You can also try counting your breaths or visualizing a peaceful image to help you stay focused on your breath.

– Incorporating Mindful Breathing into Daily Life: Incorporating mindful breathing into daily life can be as simple as taking a few deep breaths whenever you need to reduce stress or calm the mind. You can also set aside time each day for a longer mindful breathing practice, or incorporate breathing exercises into your yoga or meditation practice.

– The Power of Mindful Breathing: The power of mindful breathing lies in its ability to bring our awareness to the present moment and quiet the mind, reducing the impact of negative thoughts and emotions. By focusing on the breath, we can cultivate a sense of inner peace and well-being, and reduce stress and anxiety.

– Combining Mindful Breathing with Other Practices: Mindful breathing can also be combined with other practices, such as mindfulness meditation, yoga, or guided visualization, to further enhance its benefits. By incorporating mindful breathing into your daily life, you can cultivate a sense of inner peace and well-being, and experience the many benefits that come with it.

10: MINDFUL BREATHING: A SIMPLE BUT EFFECTIVE PRACTICE FOR INNER PEACE

Conclusion:

Mindful breathing is a simple but powerful practice that can have a profound impact on our well-being and inner peace. By focusing on the breath, we can quiet the mind, reduce stress and anxiety, and cultivate a sense of calm and inner peace. Whether you are looking to reduce stress, improve focus and concentration, or simply find a sense of inner peace, mindful breathing is a practice that is accessible to everyone, and can be incorporated into your daily life in a variety of ways.

So, take some time today to try mindful breathing for yourself, and experience the many benefits that come with this simple but powerful practice. By incorporating mindful breathing into your daily life, you can cultivate inner peace, reduce stress and anxiety, and find balance and fulfillment in your life.

11: Mindful Movement: How Exercise Can Improve Your Mental Health

Introduction:

Mindful movement, or the practice of combining physical exercise with mindfulness, is an effective way to improve both physical and mental health. In this chapter, we will explore the benefits of mindful movement, and how incorporating exercise into your daily routine can help you cultivate inner peace, reduce stress, and improve your overall well-being.

– The Benefits of Mindful Movement: Regular exercise has been shown to have a number of benefits for our physical and mental health, including reduced stress and anxiety, improved sleep, and increased feelings of well-being. When combined with mindfulness, the benefits of exercise can be even greater, as we are able to focus on the present moment and cultivate a sense of inner peace and calm.

– The Mind-Body Connection: The connection between our physical and mental health is well-established, and regular exercise has been shown to have a positive impact on our mental health, reducing stress, anxiety, and depression. When we exercise mindfully, we can also improve our body awareness, helping us to better understand and manage our emotions.

– Finding the Right Exercise for You: The best form of exercise is the one that you will actually do, so it's important to find an activity that you enjoy. This could be anything from going for a walk, to practicing yoga, to participating in a sport. The key is to find an activity that you enjoy and that you can incorporate into your daily routine.

– Incorporating Mindful Movement into Daily Life: Incorporating mindful movement into your daily life can be as simple as taking a few minutes each day to focus on your breathing and body while you exercise. You can also try combining mindfulness with other forms of physical activity, such as yoga or tai chi, to further enhance its benefits.

– The Power of Mindful Movement: The power of mindful movement lies in its ability to bring our awareness to the present moment, reducing stress and anxiety, and improving our physical and mental health. By focusing on our breath and body while we exercise, we can cultivate a sense of inner peace and well-being, and improve our overall quality of life.

Conclusion:

Mindful movement is a powerful tool for improving both physical and mental health, reducing stress and anxiety, and cultivating inner peace. Whether you are looking to improve your physical fitness, reduce stress, or simply find a sense of inner peace, incorporating mindful movement into your daily routine can help you achieve your goals.

So, take some time today to get moving, and experience the many benefits that come with combining mindfulness and exercise. By incorporating mindful movement into your daily life, you can improve your physical and mental health, reduce stress, and cultivate inner peace and happiness.

12: Meditation: Techniques for Calming the Mind and Finding Inner Peace

Introduction:

Meditation is a powerful tool for cultivating inner peace and reducing stress and anxiety. In this chapter, we will explore the benefits of meditation, and provide an overview of some of the most common meditation techniques that can help you calm your mind, reduce stress, and find inner peace.

– The Benefits of Meditation: Meditation has been shown to have a number of benefits for our mental and physical health, including reducing stress and anxiety, improving sleep, and increasing feelings of well-being. Regular meditation can also help to calm the mind, improve focus and concentration, and reduce symptoms of depression and anxiety.

– Understanding Meditation: Meditation is a practice that involves focusing the mind on a particular object, sound, or sensation, and allowing thoughts to come and go without becoming attached to them. By practicing meditation, we can train our minds to become more calm and focused, reducing stress and anxiety, and improving our overall well-being.

– Common Meditation Techniques: There are many different meditation techniques to choose from, each with its own unique benefits and focus. Some of the most common meditation techniques include mindfulness meditation, loving-kindness meditation, body scan meditation, and guided meditation. It is important to find the technique that works best for you and to make it a regular part of your routine.

– Incorporating Meditation into Daily Life: Incorporating meditation into your daily life can be as simple as taking a few minutes each day to focus on your breath and body. You can meditate first thing in the morning, before bed, or at any other time that works best for you. The key is to make meditation a regular part of your routine, so that you can experience its full benefits.

– Overcoming Common Challenges: While meditation can be an effective tool for reducing stress and cultivating inner peace, it can also be challenging at times. Some common challenges include difficulty focusing the mind, boredom, and distractions. However, with practice and perseverance, these challenges can be overcome, and the benefits of meditation can be experienced.

Conclusion:

Meditation is a powerful tool for cultivating inner peace and reducing stress and anxiety. By practicing meditation regularly, you can train your mind to become more calm and focused, improving your overall well-being, and reducing symptoms of stress and anxiety.

So, take some time today to explore the many benefits of meditation, and start incorporating this powerful tool into your daily routine. With time and practice, you will begin to experience the full benefits of meditation, including reduced stress, increased feelings of well-being, and a sense of inner peace and happiness.

13: The Art of Mindful Listening: How to Connect with Others on a Deeper Level

In our fast-paced and often chaotic world, it can be easy to get caught up in our own thoughts and concerns. We may find ourselves thinking about our to-do list while someone is talking to us, or thinking about our response while someone is sharing their thoughts and feelings with us. This kind of inattentive listening can lead to misunderstandings, conflicts, and missed opportunities for connection and growth. Mindful listening, on the other hand, is a powerful tool for enhancing relationships, improving communication, and promoting inner peace and happiness.

So what is mindful listening, and how can we practice it in our daily lives? Mindful listening is the act of being fully present and attentive to the person who is speaking to us. This means putting aside our own thoughts, concerns, and distractions, and fully focusing on the other person. It involves actively listening to what they are saying, both verbally and non-verbally, and being open to their perspective, feelings, and needs.

13: THE ART OF MINDFUL LISTENING: HOW TO CONNECT WITH OTHERS ON A DEEPER LEVEL

There are several key components to mindful listening. First, it requires an attitude of curiosity and non-judgment. When we approach someone with an open and curious mind, we are less likely to react to what they are saying and more likely to truly understand their point of view. This can be especially important in situations where there are differences of opinion or conflicting views.

Second, mindful listening involves paying attention to the speaker's body language and non-verbal cues. These cues can often provide valuable information about what the speaker is really thinking and feeling, even if they are not explicitly stated. By being mindful of these cues, we can gain a deeper understanding of the speaker's perspective, and respond in a way that is supportive and empathetic.

Third, mindful listening requires active engagement. This means asking questions, offering support, and summarizing what the speaker has said to show that you are paying attention and understanding. This kind of active engagement helps to build trust and deepen the connection between the listener and speaker.

Finally, mindful listening requires a commitment to being

fully present in the moment. This means letting go of our own thoughts and concerns, and fully focusing on the other person. This can be challenging, especially in a world that is constantly vying for our attention, but with practice, it can become a natural and powerful part of our communication style.

Incorporating mindful listening into your daily life can have numerous benefits, both for yourself and for others. By being fully present and attentive, you can build stronger, more meaningful relationships with the people in your life. You can also improve communication and reduce conflicts, as you are more likely to understand others and they are more likely to understand you. Additionally, practicing mindful listening can help to promote inner peace and happiness, as you are more likely to be present in the moment and less likely to be distracted by your own thoughts and concerns.

In conclusion, the art of mindful listening is a powerful tool for cultivating inner peace and happiness. By being fully present and attentive to the people in our lives, we can build stronger, more meaningful relationships, improve communication, and deepen our connection with others. By practicing mindful listening, we can not only benefit ourselves, but also make a positive impact on the world around us.

14: Mindful Eating: How to Nourish Your Body and Soul

Mindful eating is a practice that involves paying attention to the present moment and being mindful of the experience of eating. It is a way to connect with your body, nourish your soul, and cultivate inner peace. The idea behind mindful eating is to slow down, be present, and fully engage in the act of eating. This practice can help you to become more aware of your hunger cues, better understand your body's needs, and make healthier food choices.

One of the key benefits of mindful eating is that it can help you to reduce stress and anxiety. When we eat mindfully, we focus on the present moment and pay attention to our food. This helps to reduce distractions and distractions from external stressors, allowing us to relax and enjoy our meal. By reducing stress and anxiety, mindful eating can help to improve our overall mental health and well-being.

Another benefit of mindful eating is that it can help you to develop a healthier relationship with food. When you eat mindfully, you become more aware of the physical sensations and emotions that are associated with eating. This awareness can help you to understand why you eat certain foods and what triggers you to overeat. By becoming more mindful of these patterns, you can work to change them and develop a healthier relationship with food.

In addition to the psychological benefits, mindful eating can also have physical health benefits. By paying attention to your hunger cues and eating until you are satisfied, you are less likely to overeat and more likely to maintain a healthy weight. Mindful eating can also help to reduce the risk of developing certain health conditions, such as heart disease, high blood pressure, and type 2 diabetes.

To practice mindful eating, start by finding a quiet, peaceful place to eat your meal. Turn off all distractions, such as your phone and TV, and focus on your food. Take your time to savor each bite, paying attention to the flavors, textures, and smells. Try to slow down and chew your food thoroughly.

It is also important to be mindful of your emotions while eating. If you find yourself feeling anxious or stressed, take a moment to breathe deeply and calm yourself before continuing to eat. Pay attention to any thoughts or emotions that come up as you eat, and try to acknowledge them without judgment.

Mindful eating is a simple but powerful practice that can help you to connect with your body, reduce stress and anxiety, and cultivate inner peace. By incorporating mindful eating into your daily routine, you can improve your overall well-being and live a more fulfilling life.

15: Mindful Sleeping: How to Get a Good Night's Rest and Enhance Inner Peace

Getting a good night's rest is crucial for our physical, mental, and emotional well-being. Yet, many people struggle with sleep problems such as insomnia, sleep apnea, and restless nights. Mindful sleeping is a technique that can help you cultivate inner peace and improve the quality of your sleep. By incorporating mindfulness into your bedtime routine, you can train your mind and body to relax and release the stress of the day, leading to a more restful night.

One of the key aspects of mindful sleeping is setting the intention to release any physical tension and mental stress as you drift off to sleep. As you lay in bed, focus on your breathing and feel the weight of your body sinking into the mattress. You can visualize a warm, soothing light surrounding you, and imagine that your body is completely relaxed and at peace.

Another important aspect of mindful sleeping is avoiding distractions, such as screens, that can interfere with the sleep cycle. The blue light emitted by electronic devices such as phones, computers, and televisions can suppress the release of melatonin, the hormone that regulates sleep. It's best to avoid screens for at least an hour before bedtime, and instead engage in activities such as reading a book or listening to calming music.

In addition to setting the intention for a restful night and avoiding distractions, mindfulness can also help with sleep-related stress and anxiety. If you find that your mind is racing with thoughts and worries, try practicing mindfulness meditation for a few minutes before bedtime. Focus on your breath and let go of any thoughts or worries that arise. You can also try a body scan meditation, where you focus your attention on each part of your body, releasing any physical tension as you go.

It's also important to create a sleep-conducive environment by making sure your bedroom is quiet, cool, and dark. Use curtains or an eye mask to block out any light, and invest in a comfortable mattress and bedding to ensure that your physical needs are met.

In conclusion, mindful sleeping is a powerful technique for enhancing inner peace and improving the quality of your sleep. By setting the intention for a restful night, avoiding distractions, and incorporating mindfulness into your bed-time routine, you can train your mind and body to relax, leading to a more peaceful and restful night's sleep. With regular practice, you'll find that you wake up feeling re-freshed, energized, and ready to face the day with inner peace and happiness.

16: Creating a Mindful Environment: Surrounding Yourself with Positive Energy

In order to cultivate a life of inner peace and happiness, it is important to create a mindful environment that nurtures and supports your well-being. The space in which you live and work can greatly impact your mental and emotional state, so it is essential to surround yourself with positive energy and create an environment that promotes relaxation and calmness.

One way to create a mindful environment is by decluttering and organizing your space. Having a cluttered and disorganized environment can contribute to feelings of stress and anxiety, while having a clean and organized space can help you feel more calm and centered. Consider getting rid of items that no longer serve you, and organize the items that remain in a way that makes sense to you.

Another way to create a mindful environment is by incorporating plants and nature into your space. Studies have shown that being in nature or even just being around plants can have a positive impact on your mental health and help to reduce stress and anxiety. Adding plants to your home or office can help to create a calming and peaceful environment, and can also improve air quality.

It is also important to consider the colors and lighting in your environment. Certain colors can have a significant impact on your mood and emotions. For example, blue and green are known to have a calming effect, while red and orange can be energizing. Good lighting can also help to improve your mood and create a positive environment. Try to maximize natural light during the day, and use soft lighting in the evenings to create a relaxing and peaceful atmosphere.

Another way to create a mindful environment is by incorporating elements of mindfulness and meditation into your space. This can be as simple as setting up a quiet corner where you can sit and meditate, or incorporating symbols or images that have personal meaning and significance to you. You can also create a relaxing and peaceful environment by adding soft music or ambient sounds, or by incorporating aromatherapy into your space with essential oils or scented candles.

16: CREATING A MINDFUL ENVIRONMENT: SUR-ROUNDING YOURSELF WITH POSITIVE ENERGY

Finally, it is important to be intentional about the things you bring into your environment, and to surround yourself with positive energy. This includes the books you read, the TV shows you watch, and the people you spend time with. By being intentional about what you allow into your environment, you can cultivate a space that promotes inner peace and happiness, and helps you to live a more mindful and fulfilling life.

In conclusion, creating a mindful environment is an essential aspect of cultivating inner peace and happiness. By decluttering and organizing your space, incorporating nature and plants, choosing colors and lighting that promote relaxation, incorporating elements of mindfulness into your environment, and being intentional about the things you bring into your life, you can create a space that supports and nurtures your well-being and helps you to live a life of inner peace and happiness.

17: Mindful Parenting: Raising Children with Emotional Intelligence

Raising children is one of the most rewarding experiences one can have, but it can also be one of the most challenging. Children are constantly learning and growing, and as a parent, you play a significant role in shaping their lives and helping them develop into happy, well-rounded individuals. One of the most powerful ways to do this is by teaching your children the principles of mindfulness and emotional mastery. By fostering these skills in your children, you can help them cultivate inner peace, build resilience, and grow into happy, healthy adults.

Mindful parenting starts with being present and attentive to your children. This means putting aside distractions and fully engaging with your children, whether that be through conversation, play, or simply being there for them. It's also important to listen to your children and understand their needs and feelings. By truly listening and being there for them, you help your children feel seen, heard, and valued, which in turn strengthens your relationship with them.

17: MINDFUL PARENTING: RAISING CHILDREN WITH EMOTIONAL INTELLIGENCE

Another important aspect of mindful parenting is teaching your children the power of mindfulness and emotional mastery. This can be done through modeling the behaviors and attitudes you want your children to emulate. For example, if you want your children to be mindful and calm, you should exhibit those qualities yourself. You can also teach your children specific techniques for mindfulness and emotional mastery, such as deep breathing, mindfulness meditation, and gratitude practices.

It's also important to support your children as they navigate their emotions. Children can often feel overwhelmed by their emotions, especially as they encounter new and difficult situations. As a parent, you can help your children by being there for them, validating their feelings, and helping them find healthy ways to cope with their emotions.

One powerful tool for fostering emotional intelligence in children is through mindful communication. Encourage your children to express their thoughts and feelings, and listen to them without judgment. You can also help your children understand the perspectives of others by teaching them empathy and active listening skills.

Finally, it's important to create a positive and supportive environment for your children. This can involve creating a structured and predictable routine, reducing stress and distractions, and encouraging positive interactions and relationships with others. By creating a supportive environment for your children, you can help them feel safe, secure, and confident, which will in turn help them cultivate inner peace and emotional mastery.

In conclusion, mindful parenting is a powerful tool for helping your children cultivate inner peace, build resilience, and grow into happy, healthy adults. By being present and attentive, modeling positive behaviors, supporting your children through their emotions, fostering emotional intelligence, and creating a positive environment, you can help your children develop the skills and attitudes they need to lead fulfilling lives.

18: Mindful Relationships: Building Strong and Healthy Connections with Loved Ones

Relationships are an important part of our lives, providing us with love, support, and a sense of belonging. However, relationships can also be a source of stress and conflict, which can have a negative impact on our mental and emotional well-being. In order to cultivate inner peace and happiness, it's important to learn how to cultivate mindful relationships.

Mindful relationships are built on the foundation of emotional intelligence and communication skills. When you're in a mindful relationship, you are able to express yourself honestly, listen actively, and respond with compassion and empathy. This creates a safe and supportive environment where both partners can grow and thrive.

Here are some tips for building mindful relationships:

− Practice active listening: When you're in a conversation with someone, give them your full attention. Listen to what they have to say, and try to understand their perspective. This helps build trust and creates a deeper connection.

18: MINDFUL RELATIONSHIPS: BUILDING STRONG AND HEALTHY CONNECTIONS WITH LOVED ONES

– Express yourself honestly: When you're in a mindful relationship, you're able to express yourself freely and honestly. This helps you to be true to yourself and maintain a strong connection with your partner.

– Respond with empathy: When your partner is upset or distressed, it's important to respond with empathy and understanding. This helps to validate their feelings and creates a supportive environment.

– Communicate regularly: Regular communication is key to building a strong and healthy relationship. Take the time to talk to your partner about your thoughts, feelings, and concerns. This helps to deepen your connection and maintain a positive and supportive relationship.

– Practice mindfulness: Mindfulness is a powerful tool for creating inner peace and emotional mastery. When you're in a mindful relationship, you're able to be present in the moment and fully engage with your partner.

In conclusion, mindful relationships are essential for cultivating inner peace and happiness. By practicing active listening, expressing yourself honestly, responding with empathy, communicating regularly, and practicing mindfulness, you can build strong and healthy relationships with your loved ones. These relationships provide a source of love, support, and fulfillment, and help you to cultivate a life of inner peace and happiness.

19: Mindful Leadership: How Emotional Intelligence Can Improve Your Workplace

Leadership is an essential aspect of professional success, and it requires a combination of skills, including emotional intelligence, empathy, and mindfulness. Emotional intelligence refers to the ability to identify and manage one's own emotions and the emotions of others. Mindfulness, on the other hand, is the practice of paying attention to the present moment, non-judgmentally, and with a sense of curiosity and compassion. When these two skills are combined, leaders can create a work environment that is supportive, respectful, and productive. In this chapter, we will explore how mindfulness and emotional intelligence can improve your workplace, and how you can develop these skills to become a more effective leader.

Mindful leaders understand that their thoughts and emotions can affect not only their own well-being, but also the well-being of those around them. They are aware of their impact on others and work to cultivate a positive, supportive work environment. Mindful leaders are also able to regulate their own emotions, which helps them stay calm and focused even in challenging situations. This emotional regulation also helps them communicate more effectively and make decisions that are in the best interest of their team and the organization.

In addition to emotional regulation, mindful leaders are also skilled in empathy. They are able to put themselves in their team members' shoes and understand their perspectives, which helps them build stronger relationships and foster a sense of teamwork. When team members feel heard and valued, they are more motivated to contribute their best work, and the work environment is more positive overall.

Mindful leadership is also beneficial for reducing stress and promoting well-being in the workplace. Mindful leaders understand the importance of self-care, and they encourage their team members to take care of their mental and physical health. By promoting a culture of mindfulness, leaders can help reduce burnout and promote a healthier work-life balance for their team members.

To develop your skills in mindful leadership, start by practicing mindfulness and emotional intelligence in your own life. Pay attention to your thoughts and emotions, and work to regulate them in a healthy way. Engage in activities that promote well-being, such as exercise, meditation, or yoga, and make time for self-reflection and self-care. You can also seek out training and development opportunities that focus on mindfulness and emotional intelligence, such as workshops or coaching.

Another important aspect of mindful leadership is leading by example. If you want to foster a culture of mindfulness in your workplace, you must model the behavior you hope to see in others. Encourage your team members to take breaks, prioritize self-care, and communicate openly and honestly. When conflicts arise, take a mindful approach to resolving them, and work to create a positive resolution that benefits everyone involved.

Finally, it's important to recognize that developing mindfulness and emotional intelligence takes time and practice. Be patient with yourself and your team members, and continue to seek out opportunities for growth and development. With time, you will see the benefits of mindful leadership in your workplace, including increased productivity, improved relationships, and a more positive work environment.

19: MINDFUL LEADERSHIP: HOW EMOTIONAL INTELLIGENCE CAN IMPROVE YOUR WORKPLACE

In conclusion, mindfulness and emotional intelligence are critical skills for leaders who want to cultivate a work environment that is supportive, productive, and fulfilling. By paying attention to the present moment, regulating your emotions, and building empathetic relationships, you can become a more effective leader and promote a sense of inner peace and happiness in your workplace.

20: Mindful Communication: How to Effectively Express Your Thoughts and Feelings

Communication is a vital aspect of our daily lives and is critical to establishing and maintaining healthy relationships with others. It is not only about conveying information but also about expressing our thoughts, feelings, and emotions effectively. Effective communication is the key to building trust and fostering positive connections with those around us, and it is an essential component of cultivating inner peace and happiness. However, for many people, communicating effectively can be a challenge. In this chapter, we will explore the power of mindful communication and how it can help us effectively express ourselves and connect with others in a meaningful way.

One of the fundamental principles of mindful communication is the idea of being present in the moment. When we are present, we are able to fully focus on what is being said and respond in a way that is authentic and genuine. We are able to listen actively and to understand the perspective of the other person, and to communicate our own thoughts and feelings in a clear and concise manner. By being mindful in our communication, we can avoid misunderstandings and conflicts, and build stronger, more meaningful relationships with those around us.

Another important aspect of mindful communication is being aware of our own thoughts and emotions. When we are in touch with our own feelings and thoughts, we are able to communicate more effectively, and we are less likely to react impulsively or in a way that might harm the relationship. We are also able to better understand the perspectives of others and to respond to their needs in a way that is supportive and empathetic.

In order to cultivate mindful communication, it is important to practice active listening. This means fully engaging with the other person, paying attention to what they are saying, and avoiding distractions such as checking our phones or thinking about what we are going to say next. By actively listening, we are able to better understand the other person's point of view and respond in a way that is meaningful and supportive.

Another effective technique for improving communication is to use "I" statements instead of "you" statements. For example, instead of saying "You're always late," you might say "I feel frustrated when I have to wait for you because it makes me feel like you don't respect my time." This shift in perspective allows us to express our own thoughts and feelings in a way that is non-judgmental and less likely to result in conflict.

Mindful communication also involves paying attention to our body language and tone of voice. Our body language and tone can convey important information about our thoughts and feelings, even if we are not speaking directly about them. For example, crossing our arms or speaking in a monotone voice might communicate that we are defensive or uninterested in the conversation. By paying attention to these non-verbal cues, we can communicate more effectively and avoid misunderstandings.

Finally, it is important to approach communication with an open mind and a willingness to listen. By approaching conversations with a willingness to understand and be understood, we can foster positive relationships and cultivate inner peace and happiness.

In conclusion, mindful communication is a powerful tool for

improving our relationships and cultivating inner peace and happiness. By being present in the moment, being aware of our thoughts and emotions, actively listening, using "I" statements, paying attention to body language and tone, and approaching communication with an open mind, we can effectively express ourselves and connect with others in a meaningful way. With practice, mindful communication can become a natural and intuitive part of our daily lives, allowing us to build stronger, healthier relationships and cultivate a life filled with inner peace and happiness.

21: Mindful Decision Making: Making Choices from a Place of Inner Peace

Making decisions can often be a stressful and overwhelming process. We may struggle to balance our emotions and rational thoughts, leading us to make choices that do not align with our values or goals. This is where mindful decision making can be beneficial. By incorporating mindfulness into our decision making process, we can make choices from a place of inner peace and clarity.

Mindful decision making involves being present in the moment and fully aware of our thoughts, feelings, and motivations. This allows us to make choices that are in line with our values and priorities, rather than being swayed by our emotions or outside influences.

One of the key components of mindful decision making is to slow down. When faced with a decision, it is easy to become overwhelmed and make a hasty choice. By taking a step back and taking time to reflect, we can gain a better understanding of our motivations and desires. This can help us to make a more informed decision that is in line with our values and priorities.

Another important aspect of mindful decision making is to consider all of our options. Rather than simply going with the first solution that comes to mind, we should take the time to consider all of the possibilities and weigh the pros and cons of each one. This allows us to make a choice that is well-informed and based on a full understanding of the situation.

It is also important to focus on our values and priorities when making decisions. By considering what is truly important to us, we can make choices that align with our values and lead us towards inner peace and happiness.

Incorporating mindfulness into our decision making process can also help us to reduce stress and anxiety. When we are fully present and aware of our thoughts and feelings, we are better equipped to make choices that are in line with our values and goals, which can lead to a greater sense of peace and satisfaction.

In conclusion, mindful decision making is a powerful tool for finding inner peace and happiness. By slowing down,

21: MINDFUL DECISION MAKING: MAKING CHOICES FROM A PLACE OF INNER PEACE

considering all of our options, focusing on our values and priorities, and incorporating mindfulness into the decision making process, we can make choices that align with our goals and lead us towards a life of balance and fulfillment.

22: Overcoming Stress and Anxiety: How Mindfulness Can Help

Introduction

Stress and anxiety are two common experiences that many people face in today's fast-paced world. Despite the prevalence of these emotions, many people do not know how to manage them effectively. However, mindfulness and emotional mastery can be powerful tools to help overcome stress and anxiety.

What is Stress?

Stress is the body's response to perceived threats or challenges. When a person feels threatened, the body releases hormones such as cortisol and adrenaline, which prepares the person to fight or flee. In small doses, stress can be beneficial, as it can help a person to perform at their best in challenging situations. However, long-term exposure to stress can have negative effects on a person's physical and mental health.

What is Anxiety?

Anxiety is a feeling of worry, nervousness, or unease about

something with an uncertain outcome. Unlike stress, which is a response to a specific situation, anxiety is more of a persistent and persistent sense of unease. It can also be a response to stress, as well as other life events such as financial problems, relationship issues, or health concerns.

The Mind-Body Connection

Stress and anxiety can have a significant impact on the body, as well as the mind. Chronic stress can lead to physical symptoms such as headaches, muscle tension, digestive problems, and sleep disturbances. Additionally, long-term exposure to stress and anxiety can increase the risk of developing conditions such as cardiovascular disease, depression, and anxiety disorders.

The Power of Mindfulness

Mindfulness is the practice of being present and fully engaged in the moment. When a person is mindful, they are able to observe their thoughts and emotions without judgment, and they can respond to stressful situations in a more effective and peaceful way. By practicing mindfulness regularly, a person can develop greater emotional resilience and inner peace, which can help to overcome stress and anxiety.

Mindful Breathing

Mindful breathing is a simple and effective practice for reducing stress and anxiety. By focusing on the breath, a person can calm their mind and body, and become more centered and relaxed. Mindful breathing can be done anywhere and at any time, and it only takes a few minutes to experience its benefits.

Mindful Movement

Physical activity is a powerful way to manage stress and anxiety. When a person engages in regular exercise, their body releases endorphins, which are the body's natural mood boosters. Additionally, physical activity can help to reduce tension and muscle tightness, which can be caused by chronic stress and anxiety.

Meditation

Meditation is a practice that has been used for centuries to calm the mind and achieve inner peace. When a person meditates, they focus their attention on a particular object, sound, or movement, and they allow their thoughts and emotions to simply pass by. Regular meditation can help to reduce stress and anxiety by promoting relaxation and reducing rumination.

Yoga

Yoga is a practice that combines mindfulness with physical movement. By performing specific postures and breathing exercises, a person can improve their physical and mental well-being. Additionally, yoga can help to reduce stress and anxiety by promoting relaxation and reducing muscle tension.

Conclusion

Stress and anxiety are common experiences that can have a significant impact on a person's physical and mental health. However, mindfulness and emotional mastery can be powerful tools to help overcome these emotions. By incorporating practices such as mindful breathing, movement, and meditation into daily life, a person can develop greater emotional resilience and inner peace, and improve their overall well-being.

23: Mindful Self-Care: Prioritizing Your Mental and Physical Health

Self-care is a critical component of cultivating inner peace and happiness, as it involves taking the time to prioritize our own physical and mental health. When we engage in self-care, we are sending a message to ourselves that we are worthy of love, attention, and care. This, in turn, helps us to feel more connected to ourselves and the world around us, which can have a profound impact on our overall well-being.

There are many different forms of self-care, and what works for one person may not work for another. Some popular forms of self-care include exercise, mindfulness practices, spending time in nature, reading, taking a relaxing bath, practicing yoga or meditation, getting a massage, spending time with loved ones, and engaging in creative pursuits. The key is to find what works for you and make it a regular part of your routine.

One effective way to prioritize self-care is to schedule it into your day as you would any other important appointment. Treat self-care as a non-negotiable and make it a priority, even if it means rearranging other commitments. When you consistently prioritize your self-care, you will begin to notice a positive impact on your overall well-being and emotional state.

Incorporating mindfulness into your self-care routine can be particularly effective, as it helps to increase your self-awareness and promote a sense of calm. For example, you might try taking a mindful shower, where you focus all of your attention on the sensation of the water on your skin. Or you could engage in a mindful eating practice, where you pay close attention to each bite and chew slowly, savoring the flavors and textures.

In addition to engaging in regular self-care practices, it's also important to be mindful of our self-talk and avoid self-criticism. This can be difficult, especially if we have a history of negative self-talk, but with time and practice, we can learn to be more kind and compassionate towards ourselves.

Remember, self-care is not selfish. It is an essential aspect of our overall well-being, and when we prioritize it, we are better able to show up for others and the world around us. So make self-care a priority in your life, and take the time to nurture yourself both mentally and physically. You deserve it!

In conclusion, mindful self-care is an essential component of cultivating inner peace and happiness. When we prioritize our own physical and mental health, we are sending a message to ourselves that we are worthy of love, attention, and care. This, in turn, helps us to feel more connected to ourselves and the world around us, which can have a profound impact on our overall well-being. So make self-care a regular part of your routine and watch as your inner peace and happiness grows.

24: Mindful Compassion: Cultivating Kindness and Understanding for Yourself and Others

Introduction:

Compassion is a powerful force that has the ability to transform our lives and the lives of those around us. It is a deep sense of understanding and empathy for others, and it can bring us closer to ourselves, others, and the world at large. When we practice compassion, we become more attuned to the needs of others and are better able to provide support and help when it is needed. This type of connection not only benefits those around us, but it also enhances our own inner peace and happiness. In this chapter, we will explore the benefits of mindfulness and compassion, and how these practices can help you cultivate a life of inner peace and happiness.

The Power of Mindful Compassion:

One of the key benefits of mindfulness is that it allows us to cultivate a greater sense of compassion and empathy. When we are mindful, we are able to be present in the moment and pay attention to what is happening in our own minds and bodies. This awareness helps us become more aware of the feelings, thoughts, and needs of those around us, and can help us connect with others on a deeper level.

Compassion is not just about feeling sorry for others; it is about truly understanding their experience and connecting with them on an emotional level. When we are able to connect with others in this way, we can provide support and help them navigate difficult times. This type of connection helps us feel more connected to others and to the world, and it can lead to greater feelings of inner peace and happiness.

Mindful Compassion for Yourself:

In addition to helping us connect with others, mindful compassion can also help us connect with ourselves. When we are able to be compassionate towards ourselves, we are able to better understand and accept our own emotions and experiences. This can help us reduce feelings of stress, anxiety, and depression, and can help us feel more at peace with ourselves and our lives.

One of the keys to cultivating self-compassion is to be kind and gentle with ourselves, even when we make mistakes or experience setbacks. It is also important to recognize and accept our own feelings, rather than trying to suppress or ignore them. When we are able to practice self-compassion, we are able to build a foundation of inner peace and happiness that can help us navigate life's challenges and difficulties.

Mindful Compassion in Relationships:

Another benefit of mindful compassion is that it can help us build stronger and more meaningful relationships with others. When we are able to be compassionate towards others, we are able to understand and connect with them on a deeper level. This can help us communicate more effectively, resolve conflicts more easily, and build stronger, more resilient relationships.

One of the keys to developing compassionate relationships is to listen actively and be present in the moment. When we are able to listen to others with an open mind and heart, we are able to understand their experiences and perspectives, and we are better able to provide support and help when it is needed. This type of connection can help us build stronger relationships and foster a greater sense of inner peace and happiness.

Conclusion:

In conclusion, mindful compassion is a powerful tool for cultivating inner peace and happiness. By practicing mindfulness and compassion, we are able to connect with ourselves, others, and the world on a deeper level, and we are able to build stronger, more meaningful relationships. Whether you are looking to improve your mental health, build stronger relationships, or just find a greater sense of peace and happiness, mindful compassion is a powerful tool that can help you achieve these goals. So start practicing today, and experience the power of mindful compassion for yourself.

25: Mindful Forgiveness: Letting Go of Resentment and Finding Inner Peace

Introduction

Forgiveness is a powerful tool in cultivating inner peace. It allows us to release negative emotions, such as anger, resentment, and bitterness, and to find a sense of peace within ourselves. However, forgiving others, and even ourselves, can be a difficult process. This chapter will explore the art of mindful forgiveness and how it can lead to greater inner peace.

The Importance of Forgiveness

Forgiveness is an essential aspect of mental and emotional health. Holding onto negative feelings towards others, or even ourselves, can lead to feelings of anger, bitterness, and resentment. These emotions can cause physical and mental health problems, such as high blood pressure, depression, and anxiety. Furthermore, they can also impact our relationships, as well as our ability to connect with others.

On the other hand, forgiveness can lead to a sense of liberation, allowing us to move on from negative experiences and to find inner peace. It allows us to let go of anger, bitterness, and resentment, and to see situations and people from a different perspective. This shift in perspective can lead to greater understanding, compassion, and kindness, both towards others and ourselves.

The Process of Forgiveness

Forgiveness is not a one-time event, but rather a process. It involves acknowledging and accepting the negative emotions, such as anger and resentment, that are present within us. From there, it requires a decision to let go of these emotions, and to choose a different response. This decision may involve understanding the actions of the person who caused the hurt, as well as developing compassion and understanding towards them.

Forgiving ourselves can also be a part of this process. Many of us struggle with self-forgiveness, carrying feelings of guilt and shame for past mistakes. This can be especially challenging when these mistakes have hurt others. However, self-forgiveness is just as important as forgiving others, as it allows us to release these negative emotions and to move forward with a sense of peace.

Mindful Forgiveness

Mindful forgiveness involves bringing awareness and intention to the process of forgiveness. It involves recognizing and acknowledging the negative emotions that are present, and choosing to let them go. This is done through a process of self-reflection, in which we examine our thoughts, feelings, and reactions to a situation.

One powerful tool in the practice of mindful forgiveness is meditation. This can involve sitting quietly and bringing awareness to our thoughts and feelings, or it may involve visualization exercises in which we imagine ourselves letting go of negative emotions. Additionally, journaling can also be a helpful tool, as it allows us to examine our thoughts and feelings and to reflect on the process of forgiveness.

Another aspect of mindful forgiveness is developing compassion and understanding towards the person who caused the hurt. This may involve examining their motivations, as well as the challenges and hardships they may have faced.

25: MINDFUL FORGIVENESS: LETTING GO OF RESENT-MENT AND FINDING INNER PEACE

Through this process, we can begin to see them as a complex individual, rather than simply a source of hurt and anger.

Conclusion

Forgiveness is a powerful tool in cultivating inner peace. It allows us to release negative emotions and to find a sense of peace within ourselves. Mindful forgiveness involves bringing awareness and intention to the process, and using tools such as meditation and journaling to facilitate the process. Through the practice of mindful forgiveness, we can develop greater compassion and understanding towards others, and find a deeper sense of peace and happiness.

26: Mindful Acceptance: How to Embrace Life's Challenges with Equanimity

Life is full of ups and downs, and it can be difficult to find inner peace when things don't go as planned. This is where mindful acceptance comes into play. Mindful acceptance is the practice of embracing life's challenges with equanimity, rather than trying to resist or fight them. By accepting what is, we can reduce our stress and anxiety, and cultivate inner peace and happiness.

One of the key benefits of mindful acceptance is that it helps us to see our challenges as opportunities for growth and learning, rather than as obstacles to be overcome. For example, instead of feeling stressed and frustrated when we encounter a difficult situation at work, we can take a step back, take a deep breath, and see it as a chance to develop our problem-solving skills. By approaching our challenges with this mindset, we can turn them into opportunities for personal growth and development, rather than sources of stress and anxiety.

Another benefit of mindful acceptance is that it helps us to let go of negative thoughts and emotions. When we're struggling with a difficult situation, it's easy to get caught up in negative thoughts and feelings, such as anger, frustration, and resentment. However, by practicing mindful acceptance, we can learn to observe these thoughts and emotions without judgment, and let them go. This can help us to reduce our stress and anxiety, and cultivate inner peace and happiness.

To practice mindful acceptance, it's important to develop a regular meditation practice. Meditation is a powerful tool for calming the mind and reducing stress and anxiety. By taking time to meditate each day, we can learn to observe our thoughts and emotions without judgment, and cultivate a sense of inner peace and calm.

In addition to meditation, there are many other practices that can help us to cultivate mindful acceptance. For example, practicing gratitude, journaling, and spending time in nature can all help us to cultivate a sense of inner peace and happiness.

Another way to cultivate mindful acceptance is to engage in acts of kindness and compassion. By helping others, we can

26: MINDFUL ACCEPTANCE: HOW TO EMBRACE LIFE'S CHALLENGES WITH EQUANIMITY

develop a sense of connection and purpose, and reduce our stress and anxiety. Whether it's volunteering at a local organization, donating to a charity, or simply reaching out to a friend in need, acts of kindness and compassion can help us to cultivate inner peace and happiness.

In conclusion, mindful acceptance is a powerful tool for cultivating inner peace and happiness. By embracing life's challenges with equanimity, we can reduce our stress and anxiety, and cultivate a sense of inner peace and happiness. Whether through meditation, acts of kindness and compassion, or other practices, mindful acceptance is a key component of a fulfilling and balanced life.

27: Mindful Purpose: Discovering Your Life's Meaning and Purpose

Inner peace is not just about feeling calm and relaxed, but it also involves a sense of purpose and meaning in life. When we have a clear understanding of our purpose and what drives us, it gives us a sense of direction and helps us to feel fulfilled and content.

Mindful purpose is about taking the time to reflect on what is truly important to us and what we want to achieve in our lives. It involves examining our values, goals, and aspirations, and determining what brings us joy, happiness, and a sense of fulfillment. This self-awareness allows us to make informed decisions about the direction we want our lives to take and the steps we need to take to get there.

One of the benefits of mindful purpose is that it can help us to prioritize our time and energy. When we are focused on what is truly important to us, we are more likely to make decisions that align with our values and goals. This can help us to feel more in control of our lives and less overwhelmed by external circumstances.

Another benefit of mindful purpose is that it can increase

our resilience and ability to cope with stress and challenges. When we have a clear sense of purpose, we are better equipped to handle life's setbacks and obstacles because we know what we are working towards and why it is important to us.

There are several steps you can take to cultivate mindful purpose in your life. The first step is to reflect on what is truly important to you. This might involve considering your values, your goals, and your aspirations. You can also think about what brings you joy and fulfillment, and what you want your life to look like in the future.

The next step is to set goals and make a plan to achieve them. This might involve breaking down your goals into smaller, manageable steps and setting deadlines for each one. It is important to be realistic and flexible with your goals, and to remember that they can change over time as your priorities and values evolve.

In addition to setting goals, it is also important to be mindful of the present moment and to live life with a sense of purpose and intention. This might involve taking the time to reflect on your thoughts and emotions, and to appreciate the present moment for what it is.

Finally, it is important to cultivate a sense of gratitude and appreciation for the people and experiences in your life. When we are mindful of the good things in our lives, it helps us to maintain a sense of perspective and to feel more fulfilled and content.

In conclusion, mindful purpose is a powerful tool for cultivating inner peace and happiness. By taking the time to reflect on what is important to us, setting goals, being mindful of the present moment, and cultivating gratitude and appreciation, we can find a sense of meaning and purpose in life that will bring us inner peace and happiness.

28: Mindful Creativity: Unleashing Your Inner Artist and Enhancing Inner Peace

Creativity is a fundamental part of the human experience. It is a way for us to express ourselves, to communicate our thoughts and emotions, and to connect with others. Whether we are artists, writers, musicians, or simply enjoy creating for the sake of creating, engaging in creative activities can bring us joy, peace, and fulfillment. Mindful creativity takes this experience to a whole new level by incorporating mindfulness and emotional mastery into the creative process.

Mindful creativity is about approaching creative activities with an open and present mind. It is about being fully present in the moment and allowing ourselves to be absorbed in the creative process without judgment. When we approach creativity mindfully, we tap into a deeper level of self-expression and experience greater inner peace and happiness.

To get started with mindful creativity, begin by setting aside time for your creative pursuits. This could be as little as 15 minutes a day, or as much as an hour or more. The important thing is that you make time for yourself and prioritize your creative endeavors. Then, choose an activity that you enjoy, such as painting, writing, drawing, or playing music.

As you engage in your creative activity, focus on the present moment. Pay attention to your senses, the sights, sounds, smells, and feelings that you experience. Allow yourself to be fully absorbed in the creative process, letting go of any worries or distractions. If your mind begins to wander, simply acknowledge the thoughts and bring your attention back to the present moment.

Incorporating mindfulness into your creative process can help you tap into your inner artist and bring a new level of depth and meaning to your creative endeavors. When we approach creativity mindfully, we are more able to connect with our emotions and express ourselves in a more authentic and meaningful way.

Moreover, engaging in creative activities can also have a therapeutic effect, helping us to reduce stress, manage anxiety, and improve our mental health. When we are fully absorbed in the creative process, our minds are free to wander, and we can let go of negative thoughts and feelings. This can result in greater inner peace and a deeper sense of calm.

In conclusion, incorporating mindfulness into your creative process can enhance your experience and help you find greater inner peace and happiness. By making time for your creative pursuits and approaching them mindfully, you can unleash your inner artist and connect with your deepest emotions and desires. So, don't be afraid to get creative and allow yourself to express yourself in new and meaningful ways. Your mind and soul will thank you for it.

29: Mindful Money Management: How to Find Financial Balance and Reduce Stress

Money can be a source of stress and anxiety for many people. It is not uncommon to worry about making ends meet, paying bills, and saving for the future. However, by approaching money with mindfulness, you can reduce stress and find financial balance.

Mindful money management starts with becoming aware of your relationship with money. This includes examining your beliefs, attitudes, and habits surrounding money. For example, do you view money as a source of security or as something that brings happiness? Do you spend money impulsively or do you have a plan for saving and spending? By becoming aware of these patterns, you can begin to make conscious choices about how you want to interact with money.

Another important aspect of mindful money management is setting goals. When you have a clear understanding of what you want to achieve financially, it becomes easier to make decisions that align with your goals. This might include paying off debt, saving for retirement, or building an emergency fund.

In addition to setting goals, it is also important to have a budget. A budget helps you keep track of your income and expenses, so you can make sure you are spending your money in a way that aligns with your goals. When creating a budget, it is important to be realistic and to allow room for flexibility. For example, if you know you like to go out to eat or attend cultural events, make sure to include those expenses in your budget.

Another key element of mindful money management is reducing stress. Stressful financial situations can be caused by feeling overwhelmed by debt or not knowing how to manage your finances. To reduce stress, it can be helpful to seek out support from a financial advisor, a friend, or a support group. Additionally, practicing mindfulness techniques, such as deep breathing or meditation, can help you stay calm and centered when making financial decisions.

One final aspect of mindful money management is to practice gratitude. When we are grateful for what we have, it becomes easier to make decisions that align with our values and goals. This might mean choosing to spend money on experiences rather than things, or choosing to save money for the future.

In conclusion, mindful money management is about approaching money with awareness, intention, and compassion. By setting goals, creating a budget, reducing stress, and practicing gratitude, you can find financial balance and reduce stress. By cultivating a mindful relationship with money, you can experience inner peace and happiness, even in the face of financial challenges.

30: Mindful Entrepreneurship: How Mindfulness Can Improve Your Business Success

Entrepreneurship can be a rewarding and fulfilling journey, but it can also be incredibly stressful and challenging. As a business owner, you have to constantly deal with a wide range of pressures, from managing finances to dealing with employees, suppliers, and customers. This can leave you feeling overwhelmed and stressed, and can negatively impact your mental health and overall well-being.

However, there is a solution to this challenge: mindfulness. By incorporating mindfulness into your entrepreneurial journey, you can reduce stress, increase focus and clarity, and achieve greater success in your business. In this chapter, we will explore the power of mindfulness in entrepreneurship and how it can help you achieve inner peace and happiness while also improving your business.

What is Mindfulness in Entrepreneurship?

Mindfulness in entrepreneurship refers to the practice of being fully present and attentive to the present moment, with an attitude of curiosity, openness, and non-judgment.

30: MINDFUL ENTREPRENEURSHIP: HOW MINDFUL-NESS CAN IMPROVE YOUR BUSINESS SUCCESS

It is about being aware of your thoughts, feelings, and sensations in the moment, and not getting caught up in worries about the future or regrets about the past.

In the context of entrepreneurship, mindfulness can help you to become more aware of your thoughts and emotions, so that you can make better decisions, improve your relationships with others, and cultivate greater resilience in the face of challenges. By learning to manage your thoughts and emotions in a more mindful way, you can increase your productivity and effectiveness, and achieve greater success in your business.

The Benefits of Mindful Entrepreneurship

There are many benefits to incorporating mindfulness into your entrepreneurial journey. Some of the most notable benefits include:

– Reduced Stress: By becoming more aware of your thoughts and emotions, you can learn to manage stress in a more effective way. This can help you to reduce anxiety and worry, and improve your overall mental health and well-being.

30: MINDFUL ENTREPRENEURSHIP: HOW MINDFUL-NESS CAN IMPROVE YOUR BUSINESS SUCCESS

– Increased Focus and Clarity: Mindfulness can help you to increase focus and clarity, allowing you to make better decisions and achieve your goals more effectively.

– Improved Relationships: By practicing mindfulness, you can improve your relationships with others, including employees, suppliers, and customers. This can lead to greater collaboration, teamwork, and a more positive work environment.

– Increased Resilience: Mindfulness can help you to cultivate greater resilience in the face of challenges, allowing you to bounce back from setbacks more quickly and effectively.

– Improved Decision Making: Mindfulness can help you to make better decisions by increasing your self-awareness and reducing impulsive reactions. This can lead to greater success in your business.

How to Incorporate Mindfulness into Your Entrepreneurial Journey

There are many ways to incorporate mindfulness into your entrepreneurial journey. Here are some tips to help you get started:

– Practice Mindful Meditation: One of the best ways to start practicing mindfulness is to engage in daily mindful meditation. This can help you to calm your mind, increase focus and clarity, and cultivate greater resilience in the face of challenges.

– Engage in Mindful Breathing: Throughout the day, take a few minutes to engage in mindful breathing. This can help you to reduce stress and improve focus and clarity.

– Take Mindful Breaks: Throughout the day, take mindful breaks to check in with yourself and your thoughts and emotions. This can help you to reduce stress and improve your overall well-being.

– Practice Mindful Listening: When communicating with others, practice mindful listening. This means being fully present and attentive to the person speaking, without getting caught up in your own thoughts or distractions.

31: Mindful Aging: How to Embrace the Journey of Growing Older with Inner Peace

Growing older can bring a range of emotions, from excitement about the prospect of retirement and newfound freedom, to fear of declining health and loss of independence. However, regardless of the emotions we may experience, it is important to remember that aging is a natural part of life, and that we can approach it with mindfulness, grace, and inner peace.

Mindfulness is a powerful tool that can help us cultivate a positive outlook on aging, and allow us to fully embrace the journey as it unfolds. By being present in each moment, we can appreciate the richness of our lives and the wisdom that comes with experience. We can also work through any challenges that arise, and find peace and fulfillment as we age.

In this chapter, we will explore some of the ways in which mindfulness can help us navigate the journey of aging with inner peace and happiness.

—Acceptance of Change

31: MINDFUL AGING: HOW TO EMBRACE THE JOURNEY OF GROWING OLDER WITH INNER PEACE

One of the key aspects of mindfulness is acceptance of what is, without judgment or resistance. As we age, our bodies and minds will naturally change, and it is important to accept these changes with grace and equanimity. When we resist these changes, we create stress and tension, which can further undermine our health and well-being.

However, when we practice mindfulness, we can cultivate a sense of acceptance and openness towards these changes. We can embrace the present moment, and find peace and contentment in what is. We can also find meaning and purpose in the later years of life, and make the most of the time we have left.

– Gratitude and Appreciation

Mindfulness can also help us cultivate a sense of gratitude and appreciation for the journey of aging. When we focus on what we have, rather than what we lack, we can find a sense of contentment and joy in each moment. We can also appreciate the wisdom and experiences we have gained throughout our lives, and use them to inform our future choices and decisions.

31: MINDFUL AGING: HOW TO EMBRACE THE JOURNEY OF GROWING OLDER WITH INNER PEACE

– Embracing Our Unique Paths

No two people will experience aging in exactly the same way, and this is something to be celebrated, not feared. When we practice mindfulness, we can embrace our unique paths and find joy and fulfillment in the journey. We can also cultivate a sense of connection and community with others who are aging, and find comfort and support in shared experiences.

– Cultivating Inner Peace and Happiness

Finally, mindfulness can help us cultivate inner peace and happiness as we age. When we focus on the present moment and accept what is, we can find peace and contentment in each moment. We can also work through any challenges that arise, and find meaning and purpose in the journey.

In conclusion, mindfulness is a powerful tool that can help us embrace the journey of aging with inner peace and happiness. By accepting change, cultivating gratitude and appreciation, embracing our unique paths, and finding inner peace, we can make the most of our later years, and find fulfillment and joy in each moment.

32: Mindful Spirituality: Connecting with a Higher Power for Inner Peace

As we age, many people find that they seek a deeper connection with something greater than themselves. This can often lead to a search for spiritual meaning and understanding. For many people, spirituality and religion are an important part of their lives and can bring comfort, solace, and peace. However, for others, spirituality may take on a more secular form, such as a connection to nature, a sense of wonder at the universe, or a belief in a higher power that exists beyond the tangible.

Regardless of the form it takes, spirituality can be a powerful tool for cultivating inner peace. By connecting with something greater than ourselves, we are able to put our own worries and concerns into perspective and find a sense of comfort in a world that can often be chaotic and uncertain. Mindfulness and spirituality can also complement each other, as mindfulness can help us to slow down, quiet the mind, and tune into the present moment. This can lead to a deeper connection to the spiritual aspects of life and a greater understanding of our place in the world.

32: MINDFUL SPIRITUALITY: CONNECTING WITH A HIGHER POWER FOR INNER PEACE

To begin incorporating spirituality into your mindfulness practice, you can start by setting aside time each day for quiet reflection. This can be done through meditation, prayer, or simply sitting in silence and allowing your thoughts to come and go. You may also find that participating in religious or spiritual rituals can bring a sense of peace and comfort to your life.

In addition, exploring different forms of spirituality can help you to better understand your own beliefs and values. This can include reading spiritual texts, attending spiritual workshops or retreats, or talking with others who share your beliefs. You may also find that participating in spiritual or religious communities, such as a church or temple, can provide a supportive network of people who share your values and beliefs.

Ultimately, incorporating spirituality into your mindfulness practice is a personal journey, and it is up to you to find what works best for you. By taking the time to connect with something greater than yourself, you may find that you are able to cultivate a greater sense of inner peace and fulfillment. Whether it is through meditation, prayer, or simply being in nature, take the time to connect with the spiritual aspects of your life, and allow yourself to find a deeper sense of peace and understanding.

In conclusion, mindfulness and spirituality can be powerful tools for cultivating inner peace and happiness. By embracing both, you may find that you are able to better understand yourself, your place in the world, and the meaning and purpose of your life. So take the time to explore your spiritual side, and allow yourself to connect with something greater than yourself. The journey may be challenging, but the rewards can be profound, and the inner peace and happiness that you will find will be worth every moment of effort.

33: Mindful Nature: The Benefits of Spending Time in Nature for Inner Peace

In today's fast-paced world, it's easy to get caught up in the hustle and bustle of daily life. We are constantly connected to technology, surrounded by noise and stimulation, and in many cases, disconnected from the natural world. However, taking a step back and connecting with nature has numerous benefits for our mental and emotional well-being.

Spending time in nature has been shown to have a calming effect on the mind and body. Research has found that simply being in nature, surrounded by greenery and fresh air, can help reduce symptoms of stress and anxiety. This is because it stimulates our parasympathetic nervous system, which is responsible for regulating our body's rest and relaxation response.

Nature also has a way of putting things into perspective. When we stand in awe of the majesty of a towering mountain, the vastness of an open sky, or the intricate beauty of a flower, we are reminded of our place in the world and how small our problems truly are. This sense of perspective can help us feel more grounded and at peace, reducing feelings of stress and anxiety.

In addition to providing a sense of peace and calm, nature can also help us tap into our creative side. When we spend time in nature, we are able to quiet our minds and let our thoughts flow freely. This allows us to tap into our inner creativity, helping us to think more creatively and solve problems more effectively.

Mindful nature walks, where we focus our attention on the sights, sounds, and sensations of our surroundings, can also help us become more aware and present in the moment. By focusing on the present moment and letting go of thoughts about the past or future, we can reduce feelings of stress and anxiety and cultivate a deeper sense of inner peace.

So, how can you incorporate more time in nature into your life? It's simple! Start by taking a few minutes each day to step outside and simply take in your surroundings. Pay attention to the sights, sounds, and sensations of your environment. You can also try taking a mindful nature walk, where you focus your attention on your surroundings and let go of thoughts about the past or future.

33: MINDFUL NATURE: THE BENEFITS OF SPENDING TIME IN NATURE FOR INNER PEACE

If you're looking for a longer experience, consider taking a weekend camping trip or hiking in the great outdoors. Spending time in nature can help you connect with the natural world and tap into your inner peace and well-being.

In conclusion, spending time in nature is an effective way to cultivate inner peace and improve your mental and emotional well-being. By focusing on the present moment and connecting with the natural world, you can reduce feelings of stress and anxiety, tap into your creativity, and find a deeper sense of purpose and meaning. So why not get outside and start exploring the wonders of nature today!

34: Mindful Travel: How to Find Inner Peace on the Road

Traveling can be a wonderful way to experience new cultures, meet new people, and explore new parts of the world. However, it can also be stressful, especially if you are worried about getting lost, missing flights, or having your belongings stolen. This is where mindfulness can come in handy. By being mindful, you can turn a potentially stressful situation into a peaceful and enjoyable experience.

Here are some tips on how to be mindful while traveling:

– Practice mindfulness meditation. Meditation can help you stay calm and centered, even in the midst of chaos. Before your trip, set aside some time each day to practice mindfulness meditation. This will help you get into the habit of being mindful, which will be especially useful when you are on the road.

– Be present in the moment. Instead of worrying about the future or thinking about the past, focus on the present moment. Take a few deep breaths and look around you. Observe the sights, sounds, and smells of your surroundings. By being present in the moment, you can reduce stress and anxiety and enjoy your travels to the fullest.

— Stay organized. When you are traveling, it is easy to become overwhelmed by all of the things you need to keep track of. To help reduce stress and anxiety, make a list of everything you need to do and bring with you. This will help you stay organized and ensure that you don't forget anything important.

— Make time for self-care. Traveling can be tiring, so it is important to make time for self-care. This can include taking a relaxing bath, going for a walk, or simply sitting down and reading a book. By taking care of yourself, you can recharge your batteries and stay centered and peaceful, even in the midst of a busy travel schedule.

— Connect with nature. Spending time in nature can be a great way to find inner peace while traveling. Whether it's a park, a beach, or a forest, being surrounded by nature can help you relax and reconnect with yourself. So, make time to explore the natural beauty of the places you visit and enjoy the peace and serenity that it provides.

— Keep a gratitude journal. Writing down the things you are

grateful for can help you stay positive and focused on the present moment, even when you are on the road. By keeping a gratitude journal, you can reflect on the positive aspects of your travels and cultivate a sense of inner peace and happiness.

In conclusion, mindful travel can be a great way to find inner peace and happiness, even when you are on the move. By being present in the moment, making time for self-care, and connecting with nature, you can reduce stress and anxiety and enjoy your travels to the fullest. So, start incorporating mindfulness into your travel routine today and experience the benefits for yourself!

35: Mindful Community: Building Stronger Bonds with Your Community for Inner Peace

Inner peace and happiness are not only personal journeys but also communal experiences. Our relationships with others can greatly impact our sense of well-being, and building strong bonds with our community can enhance our overall quality of life. Mindful community is about cultivating awareness and compassion in our interactions with others, and in doing so, creating more harmonious and meaningful relationships.

Building a sense of community requires effort, commitment, and an openness to connection. It is a process that requires us to put aside our individual interests and focus on the collective good. Mindfulness practices can help us cultivate the qualities of openness, empathy, and compassion that are essential to building strong and lasting relationships.

One of the best ways to build a sense of community is through volunteering and community service. Participating in community service projects not only benefits others, but also provides a sense of purpose and fulfillment to those who are involved. By actively contributing to the well-being of our community, we create stronger bonds with others and build a sense of connection and belonging.

Another way to build mindful community is through active participation in social groups and organizations. Joining clubs, religious groups, or neighborhood associations can provide opportunities for meaningful connections with others who share similar interests and values. These groups can provide a sense of belonging, support, and a sense of purpose, all of which are essential for inner peace and happiness.

Mindful communication is also an important aspect of building mindful community. When we communicate mindfully, we listen deeply and respond with empathy, without judgment or defensiveness. This type of communication creates a safe and supportive environment where people can express themselves freely and build strong bonds with others.

Finally, it is important to cultivate a sense of gratitude and appreciation for the community that surrounds us. By actively recognizing and appreciating the people, places, and experiences that make up our community, we create a deeper sense of connection and build a more positive and supportive environment.

In conclusion, building mindful community is a vital aspect of cultivating inner peace and happiness. By committing to building strong relationships, participating in social groups and organizations, practicing mindful communication, and cultivating gratitude and appreciation, we can create a more harmonious and meaningful life, both for ourselves and for those around us.

36: Conclusion: Embodying Inner Peace for a Life of Happiness and Fulfillment

In this comprehensive guide, we've explored the power of mindfulness and emotional mastery as a means to cultivate inner peace and happiness. We've covered a wide range of topics, from self-care and compassion, to forgiveness, acceptance, and purpose, to creativity, money management, entrepreneurship, aging, spirituality, nature, travel, and community. Each chapter has provided valuable insights and practical tools for bringing mindfulness into different areas of your life and experiencing greater peace and happiness.

As you reflect on the journey you've taken through this book, you may feel a sense of growth and expansion. Perhaps you've learned new techniques for managing stress, reducing negative emotions, and connecting with others. Maybe you've gained a deeper understanding of what drives you and what truly brings you joy. Or, maybe you've simply discovered a new appreciation for the beauty and wonder of the world around you.

36: CONCLUSION: EMBODYING INNER PEACE FOR A LIFE OF HAPPINESS AND FULFILLMENT

No matter what your personal journey has been, the ultimate goal of this book is to help you embody inner peace in your daily life. This means not just understanding the concept of inner peace, but actually living it and experiencing it moment-by-moment.

To embody inner peace, you must make a commitment to yourself to practice mindfulness and emotional mastery every day. This means setting aside time each day for meditation, self-reflection, and other mindfulness practices. It also means being honest with yourself about your thoughts, feelings, and behaviors, and working to transform negative patterns into positive ones.

In addition to making a commitment to your own inner peace, it's also important to cultivate strong relationships with those around you. Whether it's through building deeper connections with family and friends, joining a spiritual community, or volunteering in your local area, the power of community can help you find greater meaning and fulfillment in life.

Ultimately, embodying inner peace requires a combination of self-awareness, self-care, and connection with others. By

making these elements a priority in your life, you can experience a profound sense of peace and happiness that will sustain you in even the most challenging of times.

So, take what you've learned in this book and begin apply-
ing it in your life today. Remember that inner peace is not
something that you find, but something that you cultivate
through consistent effort and attention. But the rewards of
this effort are immeasurable, and you'll find that a life of inner peace and happiness is truly within your reach.

Thank You

As we reach the end of this book, I want to say thanks for reading this book.

I want to get this information out to as many people as possible. If you found this book helpful, I would greatly appreciate you leaving me a review. This helps others find the book as well.

Disclaimer

This document is geared towards providing exact and reliable information in regards to the topic and issue covered. The publication is sold on the idea that the publisher is not required to render an accounting, officially permitted, or otherwise, qualified services. If advice is necessary, legal, financial, medical or professional, a practiced individual in the profession should be ordered.

This information is not presented by a financial or medical practitioner and is for entertainment, educational and informational purposes only. The content is not intended as a substitute for professional medical advice, diagnosis, or treatment. Always seek the advice of your physician or other qualified health care provider with any questions you may have regarding a medical condition. Never disregard professional medical advice or delay in seeking it because of something you have read.

The information provided herein is stated to be truthful and consistent, in that any liability, in terms of inattention or otherwise, by any usage or abuse of any policies, processes, or directions contained within is the solitary and utter responsibility of the recipient reader. Under no circumstances

DISCLAIMER

will any legal responsibility or blame be held against the publisher for any reparation, damages, or monetary loss due to the information herein, either directly or indirectly.

www.ingramcontent.com/pod-product-compliance
Lightning Source LLC
Chambersburg PA
CBHW060543130626
46553CB00002B/878